Inside the Rainbow

by Farah Farooqi
Illustrations by Margeaux Lucas

"I wish we could play outside," said Tom.

"I wish it would stop raining," said Kit.

"It stopped raining!" shouted Mom. "There's a huge rainbow outside!"

"It has steps!" Dad said.

"Let's go up the steps!" shouted Kit and Tom.

They went up the red steps.

"Everything is red!" said Tom.

Dad picked an apple. Mom picked
a rose. Tom picked a berry.

"Don't step on the red ants," Kit said.

They crossed onto the orange steps.

An orange cat and bug climbed orange trees.

"We're tired of oranges," said the cat.

"Take my apple," smiled Dad.

"Here's an orange for your kindness," said the bug.

They crossed onto the yellow steps.
Yellow monkeys swung on yellow vines.
They ate yummy yellow bananas.

"Those smell sweet," said Mom.

"Take some," said a monkey.

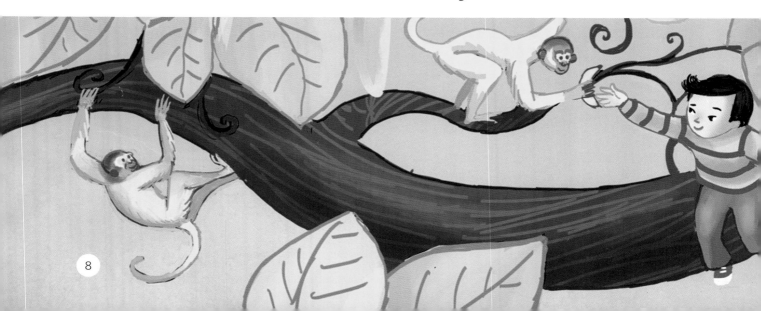

The monkey saw Mom's rose.

"We don't have red roses here,"
said the monkey.

"Take my rose," smiled Mom.

They crossed onto the green steps.

Grasshoppers hopped around. A green frog jumped onto Tom's head.

"I'm hungry," said the frog.

"Take my berry," smiled Tom.

They crossed onto the blue steps.
Blue ice was everywhere. The frog
tried to warm Tom's head.

"Let's go!" said Mom.

They crossed onto the next steps.

"This color is indigo," said Mom.
"Indigo is dark blue."

Indigo birds sang pretty songs.

"Let's thank them with our orange," said Dad.

They crossed onto the violet steps.

They played in a violet garden.

"Let's head home," Mom said.

"The steps are gone!" shouted Dad.

"We're stuck," cried Kit.

Just then, two red ants crawled out from Kit's pocket.

"You were kind to us, so now we'll help you," said the ants. "This slide will take you home."

"I can't wait until it rains again," giggled Kit.